# MINIMANUAL OF THE URBAN GUERRILLA

## Carlos Marighella

Red and Black Publishers, St Petersburg, Florida

Minimanual of the Urban Guerrilla – This translation published 1972 by the American Revolutionary Movement

Introduction © copyright 2008 by Red and Black Publishers


Library of Congress Cataloging-in-Publication Data

Marighella, Carlos.
   [Minimanual do guerrilheiro urbano. English]
   Minimanual of the urban guerrilla / Carlos Marighella.
      p. cm.
   Originally published: 1972.
   ISBN 978-1-934941-30-0
1. Guerrilla warfare. I. Title.
   U240.M34713 2008
   355.4'25--dc22

                       2008021854


Red and Black Publishers, PO Box 7542, St Petersburg, Florida, 33734
Contact us at: info@RedandBlackPublishers.com
   Printed and manufactured in the United States of America

# Contents

# Introduction

Guerrilla warfare has a long and extensive military history. While the name itself (it means "little war") dates to the French invasion of Spain in 1808, guerrilla methods of warfare have been used with varying degrees of success since before the time of Christ. The Bible mentions the Maccabaean Rebellion of 166 BC and points out that Judas Maccabaeus established a base of operations in the Judean desert, from which to launch lightning hit and run raids using lightly armed fighters. In 58 BC, the Gaullic leader Vercingetorix launched an uprising against Roman rule that lasted for almost six years. Vercingetorix depended upon small highly mobile units to destroy isolated Roman detachments and to cut off the legions' supply lines.

In the 18th century, as armies began to become dependent upon transportation systems and fixed supply lines, guerrilla warfare was practiced more often and more successfully. During the American Revolution, Francis "The Swamp Fox"

Marion took to the interior of South Carolina and held off whole units of British troops under Cornwallis and Tarleton. When Napoleon invaded Spain in 1808, bands of guerrillas led by Espoz y Mina fought on for five years, draining French resources and tying up thousands of French troops. And during the American Civil War, a band of partisans under Colonel John Singleton Mosby harassed Union armies all over the South. "Mosby's Rangers", who numbered at times less than 250 men, cut telegraph wires, decimated isolated Union forces, and even managed to capture the Union General Stoughton in his tent.

Perhaps the most famous instance of guerrilla warfare came during World War I, when a group of Arab Bedouin raiders under the command of T.E. Lawrence shot up the Turkish supply lines and pinned down large numbers of troops. The guerrilla campaign earned the amateur British soldier the moniker "Lawrence of Arabia". In 1918, the British themselves became the target of guerrillas, when Irish Republican Army "flying columns", led by Michael Collins and Cathal Brughe, forced England to grant independence to the Irish Free State.

The IRA's campaign marked a turning point in the aims and tactics of guerrilla movements. Until that time, guerrilla actions most often served as adjuncts to the actions of a regular Army, and guerrillas focused their actions on weakening an invading or occupying army so it could be defeated by a friendly army — a tradition carried on by the partisan units of World War II. After the Irish victory in 1920, however, guerrilla warfare came more and more to be viewed as an instrument of insurrection and resistance.

The earliest guerrilla "war of liberation" came in the 1910's, when Emiliano Zapata and Pancho Villa launched guerrilla uprisings in an attempt to topple the Mexican government. In the aftermath of World War II, Jewish settlers under Menachem Begin, in the British Mandate of Palestine, formed the Irgun Zvai Leumi to harass the British occupation army and establish the state of Israel. In Kenya in the 1950's, the Kikuyu tribe organized the Mau-Mau guerrillas to attempt to overthrow the

British colonial government, and in the 1960's, General George Grivas formed the guerrilla organization EOKA in an attempt to unite the island of Cyprus with the military government of Greece.

Most modern guerrilla movements—the IRA, the Zapatistas, the Irgun, the Mau-Mau, EOKA, the Kurdish rebellion, the Afghan *mujahadeen*—were traditional patriotic-nationalist movements, formed in response to local conditions and owing very little to foreign aid or ideologies. They attracted little notice from military theoreticians, and left few if any written guidelines concerning the guerrilla methods they used. It was the small number of Communist-led guerrilla movements in China, Vietnam and Latin America, however, that attracted the most attention from military authorities, and it has been the Communist-led guerrillas that have been the most vocal about theory and tactics. Since the 1960's, therefore, the word "guerrilla" has, rightly or wrongly, become almost synonymous with the word "Communist". Nearly every modern theorist on guerrilla warfare has been Leftist in orientation, and it is within this tradition that we find Carlos Marighella and the *Minimanual of the Urban Guerrilla*.

The first of the major "revolutionary guerrilla warfare" theoreticians was Mao Zedong. Mao summed up his guerrilla doctrine with the aphorism, "The enemy advances, we retreat. The enemy stops, we harass. The enemy retreats, we advance."

The Vietnamese school teacher Vo Nguyen Giap also applied the tactics of "people's war", concluding, "Is the enemy strong? One avoids him. Is the enemy weak? One attacks him." Giap's book on guerrilla strategy was entitled *People's War, People's Army*.

If one name has been indissolubly linked with the theory of guerrilla warfare, however, it has been that of Ernesto "Che" Guevara. Guevara, an Argentinean medical student, developed his guerrilla tactics during the two-year rebellion against the Batista government in Cuba, and, after the Communists seized power, put down his experiences in a booklet entitled simply *Guerrilla Warfare*.

Guevara's success inspired a number of imitators, and guerrilla movements were launched in Venezuela, Peru, Guatemala and Colombia. This wave of rural guerrilla activity, however, produced one crushing defeat after another. Guevara himself was killed while leading a team of guerrillas in Bolivia. The other guerrilla movements in Latin America were outgunned, outmaneuvered and lacked popular support, and quickly fell into oblivion.

The failure of rural guerrilla warfare sent shock waves through the militant wing of the Latin American Communist movement. It was at this time, on the brink of defeat, that Carlos Marighella, a Brazilian, recalled the strategy that had been followed by resistance movements like the IRA and the Irgun and proposed a different method of guerrilla warfare, one that depended not upon isolated bands hidden in the mountains or jungle, but on small secretive groups of fighters who operated in the large modern cities, in the very center of the government's power. Thus was born the strategy of the urban guerrilla.

## Marighella And The Brazilian Guerrillas

Carlos Marighella was born in the Brazilian state of Bahia in 1911. He was an engineering student at the Salvador Polytechnic when the Brazilian economy collapsed in 1929. Radicalized by the Depression, Marighella joined the Brazilian Communist Party.

In November 1935, the Communist Party managed to recruit several renegade Army units and staged an abortive uprising in the Brazilian towns of Natal and Recife. The uprising was quickly crushed, but it made an impression upon Marighella, who was by this time an important Party figure. In 1946, he was briefly elected to the Brazilian Congress on the Communist Party ticket, but his parliamentary career only left him more convinced that only military struggle would topple the Brazilian regime.

The Communists, however, were opposed to any armed action, preferring instead the seizure of power through political mobilization. Marighella became a constant critic of the Brazilian Communists, arguing that their byzantine political alliances and their debates over doctrinaire questions were pointless and unproductive. In 1952, Marighella was elected to the Brazilian Communist Party's Central Committee, where he continued to press for militant action.

In 1964, a coup d'etat led by Marshal Humberto Castelo Branco seized power and imposed a military government on Brazil. Civil rights were suspended and police powers were expanded. In response, Marighella resigned from the Communist Party in August 1967 to begin a guerrilla campaign to topple the regime. Marighella and the Communists would remain implacable enemies for the rest of his life.

In February 1968, Marighella organized the Acao Libertadora Nacional ("National Liberation Action"), an urban guerrilla group dedicated to the overthrow of the Brazilian military government and to the defeat of what he referred to as "North American imperialism" in Brazil. The ALN carried out a series of raids on arsenals and banks to obtain money and weapons, and then launched a full-scale urban campaign. Marighella's guerrillas ambushed Army personnel and assassinated members of the regime, but their most widely-publicized actions were the kidnapping of several foreign diplomats (including the United States Ambassador) and their exchange for captured and imprisoned guerrillas.

In 1969, after almost two years of fighting, Marighella systematized the tactics being carried out by the ALN and put them into booklet form — the *Minimanual of the Urban Guerrilla*. Shortly after, in November 1969, Marighella was surrounded by the Sao Paulo police and killed in a shootout. He was fifty-eight years old.

## Principles Of The *Minimanual*

The doctrines of urban guerrilla fighting were not new, and Marighella did not invent them in 1969. The principles set out in Marighella's *Minimanual* were well known to Cathal Brughe in 1918 and Menachem Begin in 1946. Neither Brughe nor Begin, however, ever systematically set out to record the principles and tactics of urban guerrilla fighting. The importance of the *Minimanual* lies in its being the first comprehensive account of the strategy of the urban guerrilla, written by one who had himself participated in an active guerrilla campaign and who had died in the attempt.

In the *Minimanual of the Urban Guerrilla,* Marighella set out a strategy for armed rebellion and resistance that drastically departed from the prevailing orthodoxy of guerrilla theory. A study of the principles set out in the *Minimanual* reveals a number of new strategic insights, bold new tactics and innovative organizational methods. Many of these ideas have been proven successful in combat; many others have been proven to be failures. Nevertheless, all deserve serious study by modern-day resistance fighters.

## Rural versus Urban Fighting

The most obvious innovation introduced by Marighella was his emphasis on combat and resistance in the cities and urban areas instead of the rural countryside. All previous guerrilla theorists had insisted that no guerrilla force could ever survive the repression of the regime unless it could withdraw into a secure enclave within an area of rough, inaccessible terrain. Lawrence, for example, used the vast impenetrable Arabian desert as a base from which to launch his attacks, while Marion's lightly-equipped raiders withdrew into the swamps and hills of South Carolina, where it was impossible for the heavily-laden British to follow.

Guevara, the most sophisticated of the "rural guerrilla" theorists, counseled his followers to build up a *foco*, or base, in rough mountainous jungle terrain, where they would be safe from attack by enemy forces, and to avoid the urban areas, where they would be exposed and vulnerable. "The city", Guevara flatly concluded, "is the graveyard of the guerrilla."

Marighella, by contrast, asserted that guerrillas could operate successfully even in the largest of urban areas. Rather than depending on the protection of rough terrain, Marighella built a guerrilla force that shielded itself with the obscurity of big-city life. ALN guerrillas depended on being able to suddenly appear, strike a quick blow, and vanish into a vast ocean of anonymous people, where they could not be found by the authorities.

Several practical considerations forced Marighella to adopt his urban-based strategy. The first and most obvious was the utter failure of rural guerrilla movements in Brazil. A group called the Nationalist Revolutionary Movement had attempted to set up a rural guerrilla base in the Sierra de Caparao, while another group attempted to carry out guerrilla warfare in Angra dos Reis after the 1964 coup, but both groups had been quickly and ruthlessly eliminated by the Brazilian military.

Part of the reason for the failure of the rural guerrillas, Marighella realized, was geographic. The vast Amazon rainforest and the rugged Matto Grosso in the interior of Brazil were impenetrable, and guerrilla forces could survive there for decades. These areas were, however, virtually useless to the regime. The real center of power lay in the cities of Rio de Janiero and Sao Paulo, on the coast, far from the rugged

Brazilian interior. Rural guerrillas in the jungles thus could survive only if they remained far from the center of power. On the other hand, if guerrillas were to be able to strike successfully at the regime's most important areas, they had to be prepared to live and fight in the large cities.

Marighella was also driven to urban-based warfare by the facts of Brazilian demographics. A vast majority of Brazil's population, and nearly all of its economic resources, were located in the cities, particularly the large coastal cities. Any broad-based insurrectionary movement must, then, have been prepared to operate in the large urban areas, where popular support could be found and where the resources of the regime were most vulnerable.

Marighella's break with orthodox guerrilla theory was not total, however. Even as he launched his urban uprising in Rio and Sao Paulo, Marighella concluded that the Brazilian Army could only be defeated if it was drawn into overextending itself throughout the country—if it were defeated piecemeal by a large, wide-ranging rural guerrilla force. Thus, although he preached urban guerrilla warfare, Marighella asserted that, in Brazil at least, the rural guerrilla war would be the decisive struggle. The purpose of the urban guerrillas in Brazil, he concluded, was simply to obtain the supplies, weapons and resources which would be needed by the rural resistance network, and to weaken and demoralize the Brazilian Army so much that the rural guerrillas would be able to defeat it.

Marighella stands, however, as the first person to assert that guerrillas could operate on a large scale in an urban area, a lesson that is still valid today. Successful rural guerrilla warfare of the classical type depends upon a number of factors: a thin population distribution, so the guerrillas may move about unhindered and in secret, rough inaccessible areas of terrain where the fighters can elude pursuing government forces, and a lack of roads or means of communication, which hampers the counter-insurgency efforts of the regime. Above all, rural guerrilla warfare can only be successful within a rural-based economic and social structure, in which the guerrillas can inflict crippling damage to the regime's power and resources.

While this situation held true for many nonindustrial Third World nations, it is not true for the modern industrial nations of North America, Europe or Asia. These nations are highly centralized, and are based upon an urban economic and social system. The resources and wealth of the regime are concentrated in the urban areas, as are the people upon whose support the entire guerrilla movement depends. In the industrial nations, therefore, any successful resistance network must take the form of the "urban guerrilla".

## Organization of the Guerrilla Network

Another important innovation which was introduced by Marighella concerned the structure of a clandestine guerrilla organization. Marighella had a series of arguments with the Brazilian Communists and with other guerrilla groups concerning internal organization, an argument that may best be described as being one of "centralization vs. decentralization".

The prevailing orthodoxy held that guerrilla organizations should be tightly organized with a rigid command hierarchy, so that each unit would receive its directions from a centralized command. The guerrilla commanders would decide what actions should be carried out, and orders would then be passed down the line to the actual units who would be assigned these tasks.

This structure made it easy for leaders to control the actions of the guerrillas under their command, but the system resulted less from reasons of efficiency than from the fact that most guerrilla groups are either adjuncts of a regular army (Mosby's Raiders, Lawrence of Arabia) or try to make the pretension of being an actual army (the IRA, the Irgun, EOKA). Communist guerrillas, in particular, readily adopted this pyramidical top-down structure—it was simply a modification of the traditional Leninist reliance upon the decision-makers in the all-powerful Central Committee.

Marighella, on the other hand, rejected the traditional methods of organization, and instead built up a loose network of local groups. The basic unit of Marighella's guerrilla force was the "firing group", which consisted of four or five fighters. Two or more firing groups made up a "firing team", and it was these autonomous firing teams that planned and carried out guerrilla actions.

The loose structure introduced by Marighella has several advantages for the urban guerrillas. It is extremely difficult for the state security forces to infiltrate an informer or provocateur into a unit of guerrillas that consists of only four or five people.

Small independent units also provide the compartmentalization which is necessary for security—since each unit is autonomous and doesn't know where the other units are or what they are doing, the regime's security forces can only eliminate them if they can penetrate each individual group. The decentralized network also greatly simplifies the tasks of the guerrilla leadership. Rather than keeping track of everything that every unit is doing, the guerrilla leadership need only issue general guidelines and priorities, and then leave it up to each unit to plan and carry out its own operations. Thus, guerrilla units are free to respond in an instant to changing needs or conditions, without the necessity of waiting for instructions or orders. This makes the entire guerrilla network more flexible and responsive.

The decentralized structure adopted by Marighella also eliminates a major danger faced by more traditional guerrilla movements. The top-down hierarchical organizations are very vulnerable to arrests, since if the leadership is captured or betrayed, the entire organization is decapitated and incapable of acting. Marighella's organization, however, is quite capable of continuing operations even if the leadership is lost, since each unit provides its own leadership. Rather than having the relatively simple task of finding and eliminating the resistance leadership, the regime's security forces are faced with the impossible task of hunting down dozens of independent "cells", each of which has only minimal links to the others.

## Guerrilla Tactics

Marighella divides his discussion of urban guerrilla warfare into several diverse topics, each of which is treated in detail. Some of the conclusions reached by Marighella are valid and useful even today, while others have proven to be useless or worse.

The dedication of the booklet, to several Brazilian guerrillas who died in combat, sets the tone for the entire work. Like Marighella himself, the *Minimanual* dispenses with theoretical and doctrinal speculation, and instead offers a plan of action, a method whereby people can pick up weapons, take to the streets, and fight to overthrow an intolerable regime. "What we must do," Marighella declares, "is fight."

The *Minimanual* begins with a "Definition of the Urban Guerrilla". The urban guerrilla, Marighella notes, is not a mere thrill-seeker or common criminal; an urban guerrilla is one who fights to topple a dictatorship. If war is the continuation of politics by other means, Marighella reminds us that guerrilla warfare is essentially a political struggle, not a military one.

Marighella then lists the "Personal Qualities of the Urban Guerrilla". The essence is that the guerrilla be self-confident, clever, adaptable and motivated. Only such a person is able to withstand the rigors of an underground existence.

If the urban guerrilla is to survive, Marighella notes, he must live in close contact with the population, and must seek to use his meager weapons in the most efficient and effective ways possible. The guerrilla must "live off the land", even in the city, and must obtain what he needs from his surroundings, usually by seizing them from the enemy through armed action.

The urban guerrilla must be well-trained, and must have a working knowledge of several different disciplines. Since the guerrilla is so weak compared to the forces of the regime, he must be prepared to make use of every possible advantage to help him survive.

Marighella then discusses "The Urban Guerrilla's Weapons". Like, the guerrilla himself, his weapons must be mobile but effective. The ideal urban guerrilla weapon, Marighella concluded, is the submachine gun — small, light, easily concealable, and capable of putting out tremendous firepower. Marighella also makes the important point that guerrillas should be familiar with all weapons used by the regime's forces, so captured weapons and ammunition can be utilized by the guerrillas. Marighella's guerrillas carried the INA .45 caliber submachine gun (a Brazilian copy of the Danish MADSEN). Modern guerrillas, applying Marighella's lessons, would do well with Uzi 9mm submachine guns or AR-15 rifles, with the .45 or 9mm automatic as a sidearm.

Marighella also points out that, since ammunition supplies will be limited and since hesitation can mean death, the urban guerrilla must train with his weapons religiously, until he is able to make every shot count. "The urban guerrilla's life," he concludes, "depends on shooting."


Marighella then discusses the organization and logistics of an urban guerrilla unit. The firing teams must use their firepower to obtain the weapons, ammunition, transportation and other things which they need from within the urban environment. Guerrilla logistics depend upon "expropriations" — armed seizures of supplies and equipment. These expropriations make up the bulk of the urban guerrilla's actions.

The remainder of the *Minimanual* consists of a detailed look at the various tactics and strategies of urban guerrilla combat. Marighella explains and illustrates the most basic principles of a successful guerrilla action, which can be summed up as: surprise, mobility, superior concentration of force, knowledge of the terrain, and superior intelligence and information, brought about with the cooperation of the population.

Only one area within Marighella's discussion needs further emphasis—the section on the use of "terrorism". Most of us understand the word "terrorism" to mean the kind of indiscriminate violence carried out by many groups which call themselves "freedom fighters"—airplane bombings, letter bombs, bombs planted in shopping centers or pubs. This sort of random attack is not a part of the arsenal of a serious urban resistance movement, and Marighella himself strongly condemned this sort of violence. By "terrorism", Marighella meant bombings and attacks carried out, not on the public at large, but specifically on the enemy regime. Firebombings of police stations or government offices, bomb attacks on troop barracks or arsenals, sniper attacks on government officials—all of these fall under Marighella's definition of "terrorism". Their purpose, quite simply, is to terrorize—to force the regime and its officials to live in dread under constant fear of attack.

Marighella closes his discussion of urban guerrilla tactics with a section entitled "The Seven Sins of the Urban Guerrilla". This section is well worth careful study. Nearly every guerrilla group or resistance movement that has been defeated lost not because it was outgunned or lacked firepower—it was defeated because it committed one of the seven cardinal sins set out by Marighella.

The *Minimanual* closes with a short section on "Popular Support." This section may well be the most important in the whole booklet. It cannot be emphasized strongly enough that popular support and public sympathy is the one weapon without which the guerrillas cannot succeed. Even if the guerrillas are exemplary in their organization, tactics, strategy and planning, if they lack the support of a significant portion of the population, they will be constantly betrayed and systematically hunted down and eliminated. Ultimately, it was this very lack of public support that led to Marighella's own death.

The *Minimanual* is essentially a practical handbook of urban combat, a "how-to" manual of urban guerrilla warfare. As such, it has served as a bible for resistance networks and guerrilla movements around the world, and urban guerrillas on several continents have adopted the organizational and tactical framework first set out by Marighella's *Minimanual*. Copies of the *Minimanual* have turned up in the hands of armed urban movements of every political and ideological description, including the Weathermen, the Basque ETA, the Italian Red Brigades, the German Red Army Fraction and the Provisional Irish Republican Army. The *Minimanual of the Urban Guerrilla* remains today, decades after it was written, one of the most comprehensive manuals of urban resistance ever written.


Editor, Red and Black Publishers

2008

# Minimanual of the Urban Guerrilla

## by Carlos Marighella

I would like to make a two-fold dedication of this work; first, to the memories of Edson Souto, Marco Antonio Bras de Carvalho, Melson Jose de Almeida ("Escoteiro") and so many other heroic fighters and urban guerrillas who fell at the hands of the assassins of the Military Police, the Army, the Navy, the Air Force, and the DOPS, hated instruments of the repressive military dictatorship.

Second, to the brave comrades—men and women—imprisoned in the medieval dungeons of the Brazilian Government and subjected to tortures that even surpass the horrendous crimes carried out by the Nazis. Like those comrades whose memories we revere, as well as those taken prisoner in combat, what we must do is fight.

Each comrade who opposes the military dictatorship and wants to oppose it can do something, however small the task may seem. I urge all who read this minimanual and decide that they cannot remain inactive, to follow its instructions and join the struggle now. I ask this because, under any theory and under any circumstances, the duty of every revolutionary is to make the revolution.

Another important point is not merely to read this minimanual here and now, but to circulate its contents. This circulation will be possible if those who agree with its ideas make mimeographed copies or print it in a booklet, (although in this latter case, armed struggle itself will be necessary.)

Finally, the reason why this minimanual bears my signature is that the ideas expressed or systematized here reflect the personal experiences of a group of people engaged in armed struggle in Brazil, among whom I have the honor to be included. So that certain individuals will have no doubts about what this minimanual says, and can no longer deny the facts or continue to say that the conditions for armed struggle do not exist, it is necessary to assume responsibility for what is said and done. Therefore, anonymity becomes a problem in a work like this. The important fact is that there are patriots prepared to fight like soldiers, and the more there are the better.

The accusation of "violence" or "terrorism" no longer has the negative meaning it used to have. It has aquired new clothing; a new color. It does not divide, it does not discredit; on the contrary, it represents a center of attraction. Today, to be "violent" or a "terrorist" is a quality that ennobles any honorable person, because it is an act worthy of a revolutionary engaged in armed struggle against the shameful military dictatorship and its atrocities.

Carlos Marighella

1969

# A Definition Of The Urban Guerrilla

The urban guerrilla is a person who fights the military dictatorship with weapons, using unconventional methods. A revolutionary and an ardent patriot, he is a fighter for his country's liberation, a friend of the people and of freedom. The area in which the urban guerrilla operates is in the large Brazilian cities. There are also criminals or outlaws who work in the big cities. Many times, actions by criminals are taken to be actions by urban guerrillas.

The urban guerrilla, however, differs radically from the criminal. The criminal benefits personally from his actions, and attacks indiscrimminately without distinguishing between the exploiters and the exploited, which is why there are so many ordinary people among his victims. The urban guerrilla follows a political goal, and only attacks the government, the big businesses and the foreign imperialists.

Another element just as harmful to the guerrillas as the criminal, and also operating in the urban area, is the counterrevolutionary, who creates confusion, robs banks, throws bombs, kidnaps, assassinates, and commits the worst crimes imaginable against urban guerrillas, revolutionary priests, students, and citizens who oppose tyranny and seek liberty.

The urban guerrilla is an implacable enemy of the regime, and systematically inflicts damage on the authorities and on the people who dominate the country and exercise power. The primary task of the urban guerrilla is to distract, to wear down, to demoralize the military regime and its repressive forces, and also to attack and destroy the wealth and property of the foreign managers and the Brazilian upper class.

The urban guerrilla is not afraid to dismantle and destroy the present Brazilian economic, political and social system, for his aim is to aid the rural guerrillas and to help in the creation of a totally new and revolutionary social and political structure, with the armed population in power.

## Personal Qualities Of The Urban Guerrilla

The urban guerrilla is characterized by his bravery and his decisive nature. He must be a good tactician, and a good marksman. The urban guerrilla must be a person of great cleverness to compensate for the fact that he is not sufficiently strong in weapons, ammunition and equipment.

The career military officers and the government police have modern weapons and transport, and can go about anywhere freely, using the force of their own strength. The urban guerrilla does not have such resources at his disposal, and leads a clandestine existence. The guerrilla may be a convicted person or one who is out on parole, and must then use false documents.

Nevertheless, the urban guerrilla has an advantage over the conventional military or the police. It is that, while the military and the police act on behalf of the enemy, whom the people hate, the urban guerrilla defends a just cause, which is the people's cause.

The urban guerrilla's weapons are inferior to the enemy's, but from the moral point of view, the urban guerrilla has an undeniable superiority. This moral superiority is what sustains the urban guerrilla. Thanks to it, the urban guerrilla can accomplish his principle duty, which is to attack and survive.

The urban guerrilla has to capture or steal weapons from the enemy to be able to fight. Because his weapons are not uniform—since what he has are expropriated or have fallen into his hands in various ways—the urban guerrilla faces the problem of a variety of weapons and a shortage of ammunition. Moreover, he has no place in which to practice shooting and marksmanship. These difficulties have to be overcome, forcing the urban guerrillas to be imaginative and creative—qualities without which it would be impossible for him to carry out his role as a revolutionary.

The urban guerrilla must possess initiative, mobility and flexibility, as well as versatility and a command of any situation. Initiative especially is an indispensible quality. It is not always possible to foresee everything, and the urban guerrilla cannot let himself become confused, or wait for instructions. His duty is to act, to find adequate solutions for each problem he faces, and to retreat. It is better to err acting than to do nothing for fear of making a mistake. Without initiative, there is no urban guerrilla warfare.

Other important qualities in the urban guerrilla are the following: to be a good walker, to be able to stand up against fatigue, hunger, rain or heat. To know how to hide, and how to be vigilant. To conquer the art of dissembling. Never to fear danger. To behave the same by day as by night. Not to act impetuously. To have unlimited patience. To remain calm and cool in the worst of conditions and situations. Never to leave a track or trail. Not to get discouraged.

In the face of the almost insurmountable difficulties in urban guerrilla warfare, sometimes comrades weaken and give up the fight.

The urban guerrilla is not a businessman in an urban company, nor is he an actor in a play. Urban guerrilla warfare, like rural guerrilla warfare, is a pledge which the guerrilla makes to himself. When he can no longer face the difficulties, or if he knows that he lacks the patience to wait, then it is better for him to relinquish his role before he betrays his pledge, for he clearly lacks the basic qualities necessary to be a guerrilla.

## How The Urban Guerrilla Lives

The urban guerrilla must know how to live among the people, and he must be careful not to appear strange and different from ordinary city life. He should not wear clothes that are different from those that other people wear. Elaborate and high-fashion clothing for men or women may often be a handicap if the urban guerrilla's mission takes him into working class neighborhoods, or sections where such dress is uncommon. The same care has to be taken if the urban guerrilla must move from the South of the country to the North, and vice versa.

The urban guerrilla must make his living through his job or his professional activity. If he is known and sought by the police, he must go underground, and sometimes must live hidden. Under such circumstances, the urban guerrilla cannot reveal his activity to anyone, since this information is always and only the responsibility of the revolutionary organization in which he is participating.

The urban guerrilla must have a great ability for observation. He must be well-informed about everything, particularly about the enemy's movements, and he must be very inquisitive and knowledgable about the area in which he lives, operates, or travels through.

But the fundamental characteristic of the urban guerrilla is that he is a man who fights with weapons; given these circumstances, there is very little likelihood that he will be able to follow his normal profession for long without being identified by the police. The role of expropriation thus looms as clear as high noon. It is impossible for the urban guerrilla to exist and survive without fighting to expropriate.

Thus, the armed struggle of the urban guerrilla points towards two essential objectives:

> 1. the physical elimination of the leaders and assistants of the armed forces and of the police;

> 2. the expropriation of government resources and the wealth belonging to the rich businessmen, the large landowners and the imperialists, with small expropriations used for the sustenance of the individual guerrillas and large ones for the maintenance of the revolutionary organization itself.

It is clear that the armed struggle of the urban guerrilla also has other objectives. But here we are referring to the two basic objectives, above all expropration. It is necessary for every urban guerrilla to always keep in mind that he can only maintain his existence if he is able to kill the police and those dedicated to repression, and if he is determined — truly determined — to expropriate the wealth of the rich businessmen, landowners and imperialists.

One of the fundamental characteristics of the Brazilian revolution is that, from the beginning, it developed around the expropriation of the wealth of the major business, imperialist and landowning interests, without excluding the largest and most powerful commercial elements engaged in the import-export business. And by expropriating the wealth of the principle enemies of the people, the Brazilian revolution was able to hit them at their vital center, with preferential and systematic attacks on the banking network — that is to say, the most telling blows were leveled at the businessman's nerve system.

The bank robberies carried out by the Brazilian urban guerrillas hurt big businesses and others, the foreign companies which insure and re-insure the banking capital, the imperialist companies, the federal and state governments — all of them are systematically expropriated as of now.

The fruit of these expropriations has been devoted to the tasks of learning and perfecting urban guerrilla techniques, the purchase, production and transportation of weapons and ammunition for the rural areas, the security precautions of the guerrillas, the daily maintenance of the fighters, those who have been liberated from prison by armed force, those who have been wounded, and those who are being persecuted by the police, and to any kind of problem concerning comrades liberated from jail or assassinated by the police and the military dictatorship.

The tremendous costs of the revolutionary war must fall upon the big businesses, on the imperialists, on the large landowners, and on the government too — both federal and state—since they are all exploiters and oppressors of the people. Men of the government, agents of the dictatorship and of foreign imperialism, especially, must pay with their lives for the crimes they have committed against the Brazilian people.

In Brazil, the number of violent actions carried out by urban guerrillas, including executions, explosions, seizures of weapons, ammunition and explosives, assaults on banks and prisons, etc., is significant enough to leave no room for doubt as to the actual aims of the revolutionaries; all are witnesses to the fact that we are in a full revolutionary war and that this war can be waged only by violent means.

This is the reason why the urban guerrilla uses armed struggle, and why he continues to concentrate his efforts on the physical extermination of the agents of repression, and to dedicate 24 hours a day to expropriations from the people's exploiters.

## Technical Preparation Of The Urban Guerrilla

No one can become an urban guerrilla without paying special attention to technical preparation.

The technical preparation of the urban guerrilla runs from a concern for his physical condition to a knowledge of and apprenticeship in professions and skills of all kinds, particularly manual skills.

The urban guerrilla can have a strong physical constitution only if he trains systematically. He cannot be a good fighter if he has not learned the art of fighting. For that reason, the urban guerrilla must learn and practice the various forms of unarmed fighting, of attack, and of personal defense. Other useful forms of physical preparation are hiking, camping, the practice of survival in the woods, mountain climbing, rowing, swimming, skin diving and training as a frogman, fishing, harpooning, and the hunting of birds and of small and big game.

It is very important to learn how to drive a car, pilot a plane, handle a motor boat and a sailboat, understand mechanics, radio, telephone, electricity and have some knowledge of electronics techniques. It is also important to have a knowledge of topographical information, to be able to determine one's position by instruments or other available resources, to calculate distances, make maps and plans, draw to scale, make timings, and work with an angle protractor, a compass, etc. A knowledge of chemistry, of color combination and of stamp-making, the mastery of the skills of calligraphy and the copying of letters, and other techniques are part of the technical preparation of the urban guerrilla, who is obliged to falsify documents in order to live within a society that he seeks to destroy. In the area of "makeshift" medicine, the urban guerrilla has the special role of being a doctor or understanding medicine, nursing, pharmacology, drugs, basic surgery and emergency first aid.

The basic question in the technical preparation of the urban guerrilla is, nevertheless, to know how to handle weapons such as the submachine gun, revolver, automatic pistol, FAL, various types of shotguns, carbines, mortars, bazookas, etc.

A knowledge of various types of ammunition and explosives is another aspect to consider. Among the explosives, dynamite must be well understood. The use of incendiary bombs, smoke bombs, and other types is also indispensible prior training. To know how to improvise and repair weapons, prepare Molotov cocktails, grenades, mines, homemade destructive devices, how to blow up bridges, tear up and put out of service railroads and railroad cars, these are necessities in the technical preparation of the urban guerrilla that can never be considered unimportant.

The highest level of preparation for the urban guerrilla is the training camp for technical training. But only the guerrilla who has already passed a preliminary examination can go to this school—that is to say, one who has passed the test of fire in revolutionary action, in actual combat against the enemy.

## The Urban Guerrilla's Weapons

The urban guerrilla's weapons are light arms, easily obtained, usually captured from the enemy, purchased, or made on the spot. Light weapons have the advantage of fast handling and easy transport. In general, light weapons are characterized as being short-barrelled. This includes many automatic weapons. Automatic and semi-automatic weapons considerably increase the firepower of the urban guerrilla. The disadvantage of this type of weapon, for us, is the difficulty in controlling it, resulting in wasted rounds or a wasteful use of ammunition—corrected for only by a good aim and precision firing. Men who are poorly trained convert automatic weapons into an ammunition drain.

Experience has shown that the basic weapon of the urban guerrilla is the light submachine gun. This weapon, in addition to being efficient and easy to shoot in an urban area, has the advantage of being greatly respected by the enemy. The guerrilla must thoroughly know how to handle the submachine gun, now so popular and indispensible to the Brazilian urban guerrillas.

The ideal submachine gun for the urban guerrilla is the INA .45 caliber. Other types of submachine guns of different calibers can also be used—understanding of course, the problem of ammunition. Thus, it is preferable that the manufacturing capabilities of the urban guerrillas be used for the production of one type of submachine gun, so that the ammunition to be used can be standardized. Each firing group of urban guerrillas must have a submachine gun handled by a good marksman. The other members of the group must be armed with .38 revolvers, our standard weapon. The .32 is also useful for those who want to participate. But the .38 is preferable since its impact usually puts the enemy out of action.

Hand grenades and conventional smoke bombs can also be considered light weapons, with defensive power for cover and withdrawal.

Long-barrelled weapons are more difficult for the urban guerrilla to transport, and they attract much attention because of their size. Among the long-barrelled weapons are the FAL, the Mauser guns or rifles, hunting guns such as the Winchester, and others.

Shotguns can be useful if used at close range and point blank. They are useful even for a poor shot, especially at night when precision isn't much help. A pressure airgun can be useful for training in marksmanship. Bazookas and mortars can also be used in action, but the conditions for using them have to be prepared and the people who use them must be trained.


The urban guerrilla should not attempt to base his actions on the use of heavy weapons, which have major drawbacks in a type of fighting that demands lightweight weapons to insure mobility and speed.

Homemade weapons are often as efficient as the best weapons produced in conventional factories, and even a sawed-off shotgun is a good weapon for the urban guerrilla fighter.

The urban guerrilla's role as a gunsmith has a basic importance. As a gunsmith, he takes care of the weapons, knows how to repair them, and in many cases can set up a small shop for improvising and producing effective small arms.

Experience in metallurgy and on the mechanical lathe are basic skills the urban guerrilla should incorporate into his manufacturing plans for the construction of homemade weapons. This production, and courses in explosives and sabotage, must be organized. The primary materials for practice in these courses must be obtained ahead of time, to prevent an incomplete apprenticeship—that is to say, so as to leave no room for experimentation.

Molotov cocktails, gasoline, homemade contrivances such as catapaults and mortars for firing explosives, grenades made of pipes and cans, smoke bombs, mines, conventional explosives such as dynamite and potassium chlorate, plastic explosives, gelatine capsules, and ammunition of every kind are indispensible to the success of the urban guerrilla's mission.

The methods of obtaining the necessary materials and munitions will be to buy them or to take them by force in expropriation actions specially planned and carried out. The urban guerrillas will be careful not to keep explosives and other materials that can cause accidents around for very long, but will always try to use them immediately on their intended targets.

The urban guerrilla's weapons and his ability to maintain them constitute his firepower. By taking advantage of modern weapons and introducing innovations in his firepower and in the use of certain weapons, the urban guerrilla can improve many of the tactics of urban warfare. An example of this was the innovation made by the Brazilian urban guerrillas when they introduced the use of the submachine gun in their attacks on banks.

When the massive use of uniform submachine guns becomes possible, there will be new changes in urban guerrilla warfare tactics. The firing group that utilizes uniform weapons and corresponding ammunition, with reasonable care for their maintenance, will reach a considerable level of effectiveness.

The urban guerrilla increases his effectiveness as he increases his firepower.

### The Shot; The Urban Guerrilla's Reason For Existence

The urban guerrilla's reason for existence, the basic condition in which he acts and survives, is to shoot. The urban guerrilla must know how to shoot well, because it is required by this type of combat.

In conventional warfare, combat is generally at a distance with long-range weapons. In unconventional warfare, in which urban guerrilla warfare is included, combat is at short range and often very close. To prevent his own death, the urban guerrilla must shoot first, and he cannot err in his shot. He cannot waste his ammunition because he does not possess large amounts, and so he must conserve it. Nor can he replace his ammunition quickly, since he is a part of a small team in which each guerrilla has to be able to look after himself. The urban guerrilla can lose no time, and thus has to be able to shoot at once.

One basic fact, which we want to emphasize completely, and whose importance cannot be overestimated, is that the urban guerrilla must not fire continuously, using up his ammunition. It may be that the enemy is responding to this fire precisely because he is waiting until the guerrilla's ammunition is all used up. At such a moment, without having the opportunity to replace his ammunition, the guerrilla faces a rain of enemy fire, and can be taken prisoner or killed.

In spite of the value of the surprise factor, which many times makes it unnecessary for the urban guerrilla to use his weapons, he cannot be allowed the luxury of entering combat without knowing how to shoot. And when face-to-face with the enemy, he must always be moving from one position to another, since to stay in one place makes him a fixed tarket and, as such, very vulnerable.

The urban guerrilla's life depends on shooting, on his ability to handle his weapons well and to avoid being hit. When we speak of shooting, we speak of accuracy as well. Shooting must be practiced until it becomes a reflex action on the part of the urban guerrilla. To learn how to shoot and have good aim, the urban guerrilla must train himself systematically, utilizing every practice method shooting at targets, even in amusement parks and at home.

Shooting and marksmanship are the urban guerrilla's water and air. His perfection of the art of shooting may make him a special type of urban guerrilla—that is, a sniper, a category of solitary combatant indispensible in isolated actions. The sniper knows how to shoot at close range and at long range, and his weapons are appropriate for either type of shooting.

## The Firing Group

In order to function, the urban guerrillas must be organized into small groups. A team of no more than four or five is called a firing group. A minimum of two firing groups, separated and insulated from other firing groups, directed and coordinated by one or two persons, this is what makes a firing team.

Within the firing group, there must be complete confidence among the members. The best shot, and the one who knows best how to handle the submachine gun, is the person in charge of operations.

The firing group plans and executes urban guerrilla actions, obtains and stores weapons, and studies and corrects its own tactics.

When there are tasks planned by the strategic command, these tasks take preference. But there is no such thing as a firing group without its own initiative. For this reason, it is essential to avoid any rigidity in the guerrilla organization, in order to permit the greatest possible initiative on the part of the flrlng group. The old-type hierarchy, the style of the traditional revolutionaries, doesn't exist in our organization. This means that, except for the priority of the objectives set by the strategic command, any firing group can decide to raid a bank, to kidnap or execute an agent of the dictatorship, a figure identified with the reaction, or a foreign spy, and can carry out any type of propaganda or war of nerves against the enemy, without the need to consult with the general command.

No firing group can remain inactive waiting for orders from above. Its obligation is to act. Any single urban guerrilla who wants to establish a firing group and begin action can do so, and thus becomes a part of the organization.

This method of action eliminates the need for knowing who is carrying out which actions, since there is free initiative and the only important point is to greatly increase the volume of urban guerrilla activity in order to wear out the government and force it onto the defensive.

The firing group is the instrument of organized action. Within it, guerrilla operations and tactics are planned, launched and carried through to success. The general command counts on the firing groups to carry out objectives of a strategic nature, and to do so in any part of the country. For its part, the general command helps the firing groups with their difficulties and with carrying out objectives of a strategic nature, and to do so in any part of the country.

The organization is an indestructable network of firing groups, and of coordinations among them, that functions simply and practically within a general command that also participates in attacks—an organization that exists for no other purpose than that of pure and simple revolutionary action.

## The Logistics Of The Urban Guerrilla

Conventional logistics can be expressed with the formula FFEA:

F—food

F—fuel

E—equipment

A—ammunition

Conventional logistics refer to the maintenance problems for an army or a regular armed force, transported in vehicles, with fixed bases and supply lines. Urban guerrillas, on the contrary, are not an army but small armed groups, intentionally fragmented. They have neither vehicles nor rear areas. Their supply lines are precarious and insufficient, and they have no fixed bases except in the rudimentary sense of a weapons factory within a house. While the goal of conventional logistics is to supply the war needs of the "gorillas" who are used to repress rural and urban rebellion, urban guerrilla logistics aim at sustaining operations and tactics which have nothing in common with conventional warfare and are directed against the government and foreign domination of the country.

For the urban guerrilla, who starts from nothing and who has no support at the beginning, logistics are expressed by the formula MMWAE, which is:

M—mechanization

M—money

W—weapons

A—ammunition

E—explosives

Revolutionary logistics takes mechanization as one of its bases. Nevertheless, mechanization is inseperable from the driver. The urban guerrilla driver is as important as the urban guerrilla machine gunner. Without either, the machines do not work, and the automobile, as well as the submachine gun becomes a dead thing. An experienced driver is not made in one day, and apprenticeship must begin early. Every good urban guerrilla must be a driver. As to the vehicles, the urban guerrilla must expropriate what he needs. When he already has resources, the urban guerrilla can combine the expropriation of vehicles with his other methods of acquisition.

Money, weapons, ammunition and explosives, and automobiles as well, must be expropriated. The urban guerrilla must rob banks and armories, and seize explosives and ammunition wherever he finds them.

None of these operations is carried out for just one purpose. Even when the raid is to obtain money, the weapons that the guards carry must be taken as well.

Expropriation is the first step in organizing our logistics, which itself assumes an armed and permanently mobile character.

The second step is to reinforce and expand logistics, resorting to ambushes and traps in which the enemy is surprised and his weapons, ammunition, vehicles and other resources are captured.

Once he has weapons, ammunition and explosives, one of the most serious logistics problems facing the urban guerrilla is a hiding place in which to leave the material, and appropriate means of transporting it and assembling it where it is needed. This has to be accomplished even when the enemy is alerted and has the roads blocked.

The knowledge that the urban guerrilla possesses of the terrain, and the devices he uses or is capable of using, such as scouts specially prepared and recruited for this mission, are the basic elements in solving the eternal logistics problems faced by the guerrillas.

## Characteristics Of The Urban Guerrilla's Tactics

The tactics of the urban guerrilla have the following characteristics:

1. It is an aggressive tactic, or, in other words, it has an offensive character. As is well known, defensive action means death for us. Since we are inferior to the enemy in firepower, and have neither his resources nor his power base, we cannot defend ourselves against an offensive or a concentrated attack by the "gorillas". That is the reason why our urban technique can never be permanent, can never defend a fixed base nor remain in any one spot waiting to repell the circle of repression.

2. It is a tactic of attack and rapid withdrawal, by which we preserve our forces.

3. It is a tactic that aims at the development of urban guerrilla warfare, whose function will be to wear out, demoralize and distract the enemy forces, permitting the emergence and survival of rural guerrilla warfare, which is destined to play the decisive role in the revolutionary war.

## The Initial Advantages Of The Urban Guerrilla

The dynamics of urban guerrilla warfare lie in the guerrilla's violent clash with the military and police forces of the dictatorship. In this conflict, the police have superiority. The urban guerrilla has inferior forces. The paradox is that the urban guerrilla is nevertheless the attacker.

The military and police forces, for their part, respond to the conflict by mobilizing and concentrating greatly superior forces in the pursuit and destruction of the urban guerrilla. The guerrilla can only avoid defeat if he depends on the initial advantages he has and knows how to exploit them to the end, to compensate for his weakness and lack of material.

The initial advantages are:

1. He must take the enemy by surprise.

2. He must know the terrain of the encounter.

3. He must have greater mobility and speed than the police and other repressive forces.

4. His information service must be better than the enemy's.

5. He must be in command of the situation, and demonstrate a decisiveness so great that everyone on our side is inspired and never thinks of hesitating, while on the other side the enemy is stunned and incapable of acting.

## Surprise

To compensate for his general weakness and shortage of weapons compared to the enemy, the urban guerrilla uses surprise. The enemy has no way to combat surprise and becomes confused and is destroyed.

When urban guerrilla warfare broke out in Brazil, experience proved that surprise was essential to the success of any guerrilla operation. The technique of surprise is based upon four essential requirements :

1. We know the situation of the enemy we are going to attack, usually by means of precise information and meticulous observation, while the enemy does not know he is going to be attacked and knows nothing about the attackers.

2. We know the strength of the enemy we are going to attack, and the enemy knows nothing about our strength.

3. Attacking by surprise, we save and conserve our forces, while the enemy is unable to do the same, and is left at the mercy of events.

4. We determine the time and place of the attack, fix its duration and establish its objectives. The enemy remains ignorant of all of this information.

## Knowledge Of The Terrain

The urban guerrilla's best ally is the terrain, and because this is so he must know it like the palm of his hand. To have the terrain as an ally means to know how to use with intelligence its unevenness, its high and low points, its turns, its irregularities, its fixed and secret passages, its abandoned areas, its thickets, etc., taking maximum advantage of all of this for the success of armed actions, escapes, retreats, covers, and hiding places. Impasses and narrow spots, gorges, streets under repair, police checkpoints, military zones and closed-off streets, the entrances and exits to tunnels and those that the enemy can close off, corners controlled or watched by the police, traffic lights and signals; all this must be thoroughly known and studied in order to avoid fatal errors.

Our problem is to get through and to know where and how to hide, leaving the enemy bewildered in areas he doesn't know. Being familiar with the avenues, streets, alleys, ins and outs, the corners of the urban centers, its paths and shortcuts, its empty lots, its underground passages, its pipes and sewer systems, the urban guerrilla safely crosses through the irregular and difficult terrain unfamiliar to the police, where the police can be surprised in a fatal ambush or trap at any moment.

Because he knows the terrain, the urban guerrilla can pass through it on foot, on bicycle, in a car, jeep or small truck, and never be trapped. Acting in small groups with only a few people, the guerrillas can rendezvous at a time and place determined beforehand, following up the initial attack with new guerrilla operations, or evading the police cordon and disorienting the enemy with their unexpected audacity.

It is an impossible problem for the police, in the labrynthian terrain of the urban guerrilla, to catch someone they cannot see, to repress someone they cannot catch, and to close in on someone they cannot find.


Our experience is that the ideal guerrilla is one who operates in his own city and thoroughly knows its streets, its neighborhoods, its transit problems, and its other peculiarities. The guerrilla outsider, who comes to a city whose streets are unfamiliar to him, is a weak spot, and if he is assigned certain operations, he can endanger them. To avoid grave mistakes, it is necessary for him to get to know the layout of the streets.

## Mobility And Speed

To insure a mobility and speed that the police cannot match, the urban guerrilla needs the following:

1. Mechanization

2. Knowledge of the terrain

3. A disruption or suspension of enemy transport and communications

4. Light weapons

By carefully carrying out operations that last only a few moments, and leaving the site in mechanized vehicles, the urban guerrilla beats a rapid retreat, escaping capture.

The urban guerrilla must know the way in detail, and, in this manner, must go through the schedule ahead of time as a training, to avoid entering alleyways that have no exit, or running into traffic jams, or being stopped by the Transit Department's traffic signals.

The police pursue the urban guerrilla blindly, without knowing which road he is using for his escape. While the urban guerrilla escapes quickly because he knows the terrain, the police lose the trail and give up the chase.

The urban guerrilla must launch his operations far from the logistical centers of the police. A primary advantage of this method of operation is that it places us at a reasonable distance from the possibility of capture, which facilitates our evasion.

In addition to this necessary precaution, the urban guerrilla must be concerned with the enemy's communication system. The telephone is the primary target in preventing the enemy from access to information, by knocking out his communications systems.

Even if he knows about the guerrilla operation, the enemy depends on modern transportation for his logistics support, and his vehicles necessarily lose time carrying him through the heavy traffic of the large cities. It is clear that the tangled and treacherous traffic is a disadvantage for the enemy, as it would be for us if we were not ahead of him.

If we want to have a safe margin of security and be certain to leave no tracks for the future, we can adopt the following methods:

1. Deliberately intercept the police with other vehicles, or by seemingly casual inconveniences and accidents; but in this case the vehicles in question should neither be legal nor have real license numbers

2. Obstruct the roads with fallen trees, rocks, ditches, false traffic signs, dead ends or detours, or other clever methods

3. Place homemade mines in the way of the police; use gasoline or throw Molotov cocktails to set their vehicles on fire

4. Set off a burst of submachine gun fire or weapons such as the FAL aimed at the motor and tires of the cars engaged in the pursuit

With the arrogance typical of the police and the military authorities, the enemy will come to fight us equipped with heavy guns and equipment, and with elaborate maneuvers by men armed to the teeth. The urban guerrilla must respond to this with light weapons that can be easily transported, so he can always escape with maximum speed without ever accepting open fighting. The urban guerrilla has no mission other than to attack and quickly withdraw. We would leave ourselves open to the most crushing defeats if we burdened ourselves with heavy weapons and with the tremendous weight of the ammunition necessary to use them, at the same time losing our precious gift of mobility.

When our enemy fights against us with the cavalry, we are at no disadvantage as long as we are mechanized. The automobile goes faster than the horse. From within the car, we also have the target of the mounted police, knocking him down with submachine gun and revolver fire or with Molotov cocktails and hand grenades.

On the other hand, it is not so difficult for an urban guerrilla on foot to make a target of a policeman on horseback. Moreover, ropes across the street, marbles, and cork stoppers are very efficient methods of making them both fall. The great disadvantage faced by the mounted policeman is that he presents the urban guerrilla with two excellent targets — the horse and its rider.

Apart from being faster than the horseman, the helicopter has no better chance in pursuit. If the horse is too slow compared to the urban guerrilla's automobile, the helicopter is too fast. Moving at 200 kilometers an hour, it will never succeed in hitting from above a target that is lost among the crowds and street vehicles, nor can the helicopter land in public streets in order to capture someone. At the same time, whenever it flies too low, it will be excessively vulnerable to the fire of the urban guerrillas.

# Information

The chances that the government has for discovering and destroying the urban guerrillas lessen as the power of the dictatorship's enemies becomes greater and more concentrated among the population.

This concentration of the opponents of the dictatorship plays a very important role in providing information about the actions of the police and government officials, as well as hiding the activities of the guerrillas. The enemy can also be thrown off with false information, which is worse for him because it is a tremendous waste.

By whatever means, the sources of information at the disposal of the urban guerrilla are potentially better than those of the police. The enemy is observed by the people, but he does not know who among the people transmits information to the urban guerrillas. The military and the police are hated by the people for the injustices and violence they have committed, and this facilitates obtaining information which is damaging to the activities of government agents.

Information, which is only a small segment of popular support, represents an extraordinary potential in the hands of the urban guerrilla.

The creation of an intelligence service, with an organized structure, is a basic need for us. The urban guerrilla has to have vital information about the plans and movements of the enemy; where they are, how they move, the resources of their banking network, their means of communication, and the secret activities they carry out. The reliable information passed on to the guerrillas represents a well-aimed blow at the dictatorship. The dictatorship has no way to defend itself in the face of an important leak which facilitates our destructive attacks.

The enemy also wants to know what actions we are planning so he can destroy us or prevent us from acting. In this sense, the danger of betrayal is present, and the enemy encourages betrayal and infiltrates spies into the guerrilla organization. The urban guerrilla's technique against this enemy tactic is to denounce publicly the spies, traitors, informers and provocateurs. Since our struggle takes place among the people and depends on their sympathy — while the government has a bad reputation because of its brutality, corruption and incompetence — the informers, spies, traitors and the police come to be enemies of the people, without supporters, denounced to the urban guerrillas and, in many cases, properly punished.

For his part, the urban guerrilla must not evade the duty — once he knows who the spy or informer is — of physically wiping him out. This is the proper method, approved by the people, and it minimizes considerably the incidence of infiltration or enemy spying.

For complete success in the battle against spies and informers, it is essential to organize a counter-espionage or counter-intelligence service. Nevertheless, as far as information is concerned, it cannot all be reduced to a matter of knowing the enemy's moves and avoiding the infiltration of spies. Intelligence information must be broad — it must embrace everything, including the most insignificant material. There is a technique of obtaining information, and the urban guerrilla must master it. Following this technique, intelligence information is obtained naturally, as a part of the life of the people.

The urban guerrilla, living in the midst of the population and moving about among them, must be attentive to all types of conversations and human relations, learning how to disguise his interest with great skill and judgement.

In places where people work, study, and live, it is easy to collect all kinds of information on payments, business, plans of all kinds, points of view, opinions, people's state of mind, trips, interior layout of buildings, offices and rooms, operations centers, etc.

Observation, investigation, reconnaissance, and exploration of the terrain are also excellent sources of information. The urban guerrilla never goes anywhere absentmindedly and without revolutionary precaution, always on the alert lest something occurs. Eyes and ears open, senses alert, his memory is engraved with everything necessary, now or in the future, to the continued activity of the guerrilla fighter.

Careful reading of the press with particular attention to the mass communication media, the research of accumulated data, the transmission of news and everything of note, a persistence in being informed and in informing others, all this makes up the intricate and immensely complicated question of information which gives the urban guerrilla a decisive advantage.

## Decisiveness

It is not enough for the urban guerrilla to have in his favor surprise, speed, knowledge of the terrain, and information. He must also demonstrate his command of any situation and a capacity for decisiveness, without which all other advantages will prove to be useless.

It is impossible to carry out any action, however well-planned, if the urban guerrilla turns out to be indecisive, uncertain, irresolute. Even an action successfully begun can end in defeat if command of the situation and the capacity for decision falter in the middle of the execution of the plan. When this command of the situation and a capacity for decision are absent, the void is filled with hesitation and terror. The enemy takes advantage of this failure and is able to liquidate us.

The secret of the success of any operation, simple or complex, easy or difficult, is to rely on determined men. Strictly speaking, there are no simple operations: all must be carried out with the same care taken in the most difficult, beginning with the choice of the human elements—which means relying on leadership and the capacity for decision in every situation.

One can see ahead of time whether an action will be successfull or not by the way its participants act during the preparatory period. Those who fall behind, who fail to make designated contacts, are easily confused, forget things, fail to complete the basic tasks of the work, possibly are indecisive men and can be a danger. It is better not to include them.

Decisiveness means to put into practice the plan that has been devised with determination, with audacity, and with an absolute firmness. It takes only one person who hesitates to lose all.

## Objectives Of The Guerrilla's Actions

With his tactics developed and established, the urban guerrilla trains himself in methods of action leading to attack, and, in Brazil, has the following objectives:

1. To threaten the triangle within which the Brazilian state and North American domination are maintained, a triangle whose points are Rio, Sao Paulo and Belo Horizonte, and whose base is the axis Rio—San Paulo, where the giant industrial, financial, economic, political, cultural, military, and police complex that holds the decisive power of the country is located.

2. To weaken the local militia and the security systems of the dictatorship, given the fact that we

are attacking and the "gorillas" defending, which means catching the government in a defensive position with its troops immobilized in the defense of the entire complex of national maintenance, with its ever-present fears of an attack on its strategic nerve centers, and without ever knowing where, how or when the attack will come.

3. To attack every area with many different armed groups, small in size, each self-contained and operating independently, to disperse the government forces in their pursuit of a thoroughly fragmented organization, instead of offering the dictatorship the opportunity to concentrate its forces in the destruction of one tightly organized system operating throughout the country.

4. To give proof of its combatitivenes, decision, firmness, determination, and persistence in the attack on the military dictatorship, in order to allow all rebels to follow in our example and to fight with urban guerrilla tactics. Meanwhile, the government with all of its problems, incapable of halting guerrilla actions within the cities, will lose time and suffer endless attrition, and will finally be forced to pull back its repressive forces in order to mount guard over all the banks, industries, armories, military barracks, prisons, public offices, radio and television stations, North American firms, gas storage tanks, oil refineries, ships, airplanes, ports, airports, hospitals, health centers, blood banks, stores, garages, embassies, residences of high-ranking members of the regime such as ministers and generals, police stations, official organizations, etc.

5. To increase urban guerrilla actions gradually into an endless number of surprise raids, such that the government cannot leave the urban area to pursue guerrillas in the rural interior without running the risk of abandoning the cities and permitting rebellion to increase on the coast as well as the interior of the country.

6. To force the Army and the police, their commanders and their assistants, to give up the relative comfort and tranquility of their barracks and their usual rest, for a state of fear and growing tension in the expectation of attack, or in a search for trails which vanish without a trace.

7. To avoid open battle and decisive combat with the government, limiting the struggle to brief, rapid attacks with lightning results.

8. To insure for the urban guerrilla a maximum freedom of movement and of action, without ever relinquishing the use of armed action, remaining firmly oriented towards helping the formation of rural guerrilla warfare and supporting the construction of a revolutionary army for national liberation.

**On The Types And Nature Of Missions For The Urban Guerrilla**

In order to achieve the objectives previously listed, the urban guerrilla is obliged, in his tactics, to follow missions whose nature is as different or diversified as possible. The urban guerrilla does not arbitrarily choose this or that mission. Some actions are simple; others are complicated. The inexperienced guerrilla must be gradually introduced into actions and operations which run from the simple to the complex. He begins with small missions and tasks until he becomes completely experienced.

Before any action, the urban guerrilla must think of the methods and the personnel at his disposal to carry out the mission. Operations and actions that demand the urban guerrilla's technical preparation cannot be carried out by someone who lacks the technical skill. With these precautions, the missions which the urban guerrilla can undertake are the following:

1. assaults

2. raids and penetrations

3. occupations

4. ambushes

5. street tactics

6. strikes and work stoppages

7. desertions, diversions, seizures, expropriation of weapons, ammunition and explosives

8. liberation of prisoners

9. executions

10. kidnappings

11. sabotage

12. terrorism

13. armed propaganda

14. war of nerves

**Assaults**

Assaults are the armed attacks which we make to expropriate funds, liberate prisoners, capture explosives, submachine guns, and other types of weapons and ammunition.

Assaults can take place in broad daylight or at night. Daytime assaults are made when the objective cannot be achieved at any other hour, such as the transport of money by banks, which is not done at night. Night assault is usually the most advantageous for the guerrilla. The ideal is for all assaults to take place at night, when conditions for a surprise attack are most favorable and the darkness facilitates escape and hides the identity of the participants. The urban guerrilla must prepare himself, nevertheless, to act under all conditions, daytime as well as night.

The must vulnerable targets for assaults are the following:

1. credit establishments

2. commercial and industrial enterprises, including plants for the manufacture of weapons and explosives

3. military establishments

4. commissaries and police stations

5. jails

6. government property

7. mass communications media

8. North American firms and properties

9. government vehicles, including military and police vehicles, trucks, armored vehicles, money carriers, trains, ships, and airplanes.

The assaults on businesses use the same tactics, because in every case the buildings represent a fixed target. Assaults on buildings are planned as guerrilla operations, varied according to whether they are against banks, a commercial enterprise, industries, military bases, commissaries, prisons, radio stations, warehouses for foreign firms, etc.

The assault on vehicles — money-carriers, armored vehicles, trains, ships, airplanes — are of another nature, since they are moving targets. The nature of the operation varies according to the situation and the circumstances — that is, whether the vehicle is stationary or moving. Armored cars, including military vehicles, are not immune to mines. Roadblocks, traps, ruses, interception by other vehicles, Molotov cocktails, shooting with heavy weapons, are efficient methods of assaulting vehicles. Heavy vehicles, grounded airplaces and anchored ships can be seized and their crews and guards overcome. Airplanes in flight can be hijacked by guerrilla action or by one person. Ships and trains in motion can be assaulted or captured by guerrilla operations in order to obtain weapons and ammunition or to prevent troop movements.

## The Bank Assault As Popular Mission

The most popular mission is the bank assault. In Brazil, the urban guerrillas have begun a type of organized assault on the banks as a guerrilla operation. Today, this type of assault is widely used, and has served as a sort of preliminary test for the urban guerrilla in his training in the tactics of urban guerrilla warfare.

Important innovations in the tactics of assaulting banks have developed, guaranteeing escape, the withdrawal of money, and the anonymity of those involved. Among these innovations, we cite the shooting of tires of cars to prevent pursuit, locking people in the bank bathroom, making them sit on the floor, immobilizing the bank guards and taking their weapons, forcing someone to open the safe or the strong box, and using disguises.

Attempts to install bank alarms, to use guards or electronic detection devices prove fruitless when the assault is political and is carried out according to urban guerrilla warfare techniques. This guerrilla method uses new techniques to meet the enemy's tactical changes, has access to firepower that is growing every day, becomes increasingly more experienced and more confident, and uses a larger number of guerrillas every time; all to guarantee the success of operations planned down to the last detail.

The bank assault is a typical expropriation. But, as is true with any kind of armed expropriatory action, the guerrilla is handicapped by a two-fold competition:

1. competition from the outlaw

2. competition from the right-wing counter-revolutionary

This competition produces confusion, which is reflected in the people's uncertainty. It is up to the urban guerrilla to prevent this from happening, and to accomplish this he must use two methods:

1. He must avoid the outlaw's technique, which is one of unnecessary violence and the expropriation of goods and possessions belonging to the people

2. He must use the assault for propaganda purposes at the very moment it is taking place, and later distribute material, leaflets—every possible means of explaining the objectives and the principles of the urban guerrillas, as expropriator of the government and the ruling elite.

## Raids And Penetrations

Raids and penetrations are rapid attacks on establishments located in neighborhoods, or even in the center of the city, such as small military units, commissaries, hospitals, to cause trouble, seize weapons, punish and terrorize the enemy, take reprisals, or to rescue wounded prisoners or those hospitalized under police guard. Raids and penetrations are also made on garages and depots to destroy vehicles and damage installations, especially if they are North American firms and property.

When they take place on certain stretches of highway or in certain distant neighborhoods, these raids can serve to force the enemy to move great numbers of troops, a totally useless effort since when they get there they will find nobody to fight. When they are carried out on certain houses, offices, archives or public offices, their purpose is to capture or search for secret papers and documents with which to denounce deals, compromises and the corruption of men in government, their dirty deals and criminal transactions.

Raids and penetrations are most effective if they are carried out at night.

## Occupations

Occupations are a type of attack carried out when the urban guerrilla stations himself in specific establishments and locations, for a temporary action against the enemy or for some propaganda purpose.

The occupation of factories and schools during strikes, or at other times, is a method of protest or of distracting the enemy's attention. The occupation of radio stations is for propaganda purposes.

Occupation is a highly effective model for action but, in order to prevent losses and material damage to our forces, it is always a good idea to plan on the possibility of a forced withdrawal. It must always be meticulously planned, and carried out at the opportune moment.

Occupations always have a time limit, and the swifter they are completed, the better.

## Ambush

Ambushes are attacks, typified by surprise, when the enemy is trapped on the road or when he makes a police net surrounding a house or estate. A false alarm can bring the enemy to the spot, where he falls into a trap.

The principle object of the ambush is to capture enemy weapons and to punish him with death.

Ambushes to halt passenger trains are for propaganda purposes, and, when they are troop trains, the object is to annihilate the enemy and seize his weapons.

The urban guerrilla sniper is the kind of fighter specially suited for ambush, because he can hide easily in the irregularities of the terrain, on the roofs and the tops of buildings and apartments under construction. From windows and dark places, he can take careful aim at his chosen target.

Ambush has devastating effects on the enemy, leaving him unnerved, insecure and fearful.

## Street Tactics

Street tactics are used to fight the enemy in the streets, utilizing the participation of the population against him.

In 1968, the Brazilian students used excellent street tactics against police troops, such as marching down streets against traffic and using slingshots and marbles against mounted police.

Other street tactics consist of constructing barricades; pulling up paving blocks and hurling them at the police; throwing bottles, bricks, paperweights and other projectiles at the police from the top of office and apartment buildings; using buildings and other structures for escape, for hiding and for supporting surprise attacks.

It is equally necessary to know how to respond to enemy tactics. When the police troops come wearing helmets to protect them against flying objects, we have to divide ourselves into two teams—one to attack the enemy from the front, the other to attack him in the rear—withdrawing one as the other goes into action to prevent the first from being struck by projectiles hurled by the second.

By the same token, it is important to know how to respond to the police net. When the police designate certain of their men to go into the crowd and arrest a demonstrator, a larger group of urban guerrillas must surround the police group, disarming and beating them and at the same time allowing the prisoner to escape. This urban guerrilla operation is called "the net within a net".

When the police net is formed at a school building, a factory, a place where demonstrators gather, or some other point, the urban guerrilla must not give up or allow himself to be taken by surprise. To make his net effective, the enemy is obliged to transport his troops in vehicles and special cars to occupy strategic points in the streets, in order to invade the building or chosen locale.

The urban guerrilla, for his part, must never clear a building or an area and meet in it without first knowing its exits, the way to break an encirclement, the strategic points that the police must occupy, and the roads that inevitably lead into the net, and he must hold other strategic points from which to strike at the enemy. The roads followed by police vehicles must be mined at key points along the way and at forced roadblocks. When the mines explode, the vehicles will be knocked into the air. The police will be caught in the trap and will suffer losses and be victims of an ambush.

The net must be broken by escape routes which are unknown to the police. The rigorous planning of a withdrawal is the best way to frustrate any encircling effort on the part of the enemy.

When there is no possibility of an escape plan, the urban guerrilla must not hold meetings, gatherings or do anything, since to do so will prevent him from breaking through the net which the enemy will surely try to throw around him.

Street tactics have revealed a new type of urban guerrilla who participates in mass protests. This is the type we designate as the "urban guerrilla demonstrator", who joins the crowds and participates in marches with specific and definate aims in mind. The urban guerrilla demonstrator must initiate the "net within the net", ransacking government vehicles, official cars and police vehicles before turning them over or setting fire to them, to see if any of them have money or weapons.

Snipers are very good for mass demonstrations, and along with the urban guerrilla demonstrator can play a valuable role. Hidden at strategic points, the snipers have complete success using shotguns or submachine guns, which can easily cause losses among the enemy.

## Strikes And Work Interruptions

The strike is a model of action employed by the urban guerrilla in work centers and schools to damage the enemy by stopping work and study activities. Because it is one of the weapons most feared by the exploiters and oppressors, the enemy uses tremendous firepower and incredible violence against it. The strikers are taken to prison, suffer beatings, and many of them wind up killed.

The urban guerrilla must prepare the strike in such a way as to leave no track or clue that can identify the leaders of such an action. A strike is successful when it is organized by a small group, if it is carefully prepared in secret using the most clandestine methods. Weapons, ammunition, Molotov cocktails, homemade weapons of destruction and attack, all of these must be supplied beforehand in order to meet the enemy. So that the action can do the greatest possible amount of damage, it is a good idea to study and put into effect a sabotage plan.

Strikes and study interruptions, although they are of brief duration, cause severe damage to the enemy. It is enough for them to crop up at different locations and in differing sections of the same area, disrupting daily life, occuring endlessly, one after the other, in true guerrilla fashion.

In strikes or in simple work interruptions, the urban guerrilla has recourse to the occupation or penetration of the site, or he can simply make a raid. In that case, his objective is to take captives, to capture prisoners, or to capture enemy agents and propose an exchange for arrested strikers.

In certain cases, strikes and brief work interruptions can offer an excellent opportunity for preparing ambushes or traps, whose aim is the physical destruction of the police. The basic fact is that the enemy suffers losses as well as material and moral damage, and is weakened by the action.

### Desertions, Diversions, Seizures, Expropriation Of Ammunition And Explosives

Desertion and the diversion of weapons are actions carried out in military bases, ships, military hospitals, etc. The urban guerrilla soldier or officer must desert at the most opportune moment with modern weapons and ammunition, to hand them over to the guerrillas.

One of the most opportune moments is when the urban guerrilla soldier is called upon to pursue his guerrilla comrades outside the military base. Instead of following the orders of the "gorillas", the military urban guerrilla must join the ranks of the revolutionaries by handing over the weapons and ammunition he carries, or the military vehicle he operates. The advantage of this method is that the rebels receive weapons and ammunition from the army, navy, air force, military police, civilian guard or the police without any great work, since it reaches their hands by government transportation.

Other opportunities may occur in the barracks, and the military urban guerrilla must always be alert to this. In case of carelessness on the part of commanders or in other favorable conditions—such as bureaucratic attitudes or the relaxation of discipline on the part of lieutenants or other internal personnel—the military urban guerrilla must no longer wait but must try to inform the guerrillas and desert with as large a supply of weapons as possible.

When there is no possibility of deserting with weapons and ammunition, the military urban guerrilla must engage in sabotage, starting fires and explosions in munitions dumps.

This technique of deserting with weapons and of raiding and sabotaging the military centers is the best way of wearing out and demoralizing the enemy and leaving them confused.

The urban guerrilla's purpose in disarming an individual enemy is to capture his weapons. These weapons are usually in the hands of sentinels or others whose task is guard duty. The capture of weapons may be accomplished by violent means or by cleverness and tricks or traps. When the enemy is disarmed, he must be searched for weapons other than those already taken from him. If we are careless, he can use the weapons that were not seized to shoot the urban guerrilla.

The seizure of weapons is an efficient method of aquiring submachine guns, the urban guerrilla's most important weapon. When we carry out small operations or actions to seize weapons and ammunition, the materiel captured may be for personal use or for armaments and supplies for the firing teams.

The necessity to provide firepower for the urban guerrillas is so great that, in order to take off from the zero point, we often have to purchase one weapon, divert or capture a single gun. The basic point is to begin, and to begin with a spirit of decisiveness and boldness. The possession of a single submachine gun multiplies our forces.

In a bank assault, we must be careful to seize the weapons of the bank guard. The rest of the weapons will be found with the treasurer, the bank tellers or the manager, and must also be seized. Quite often, we succeed in capturing weapons in police stations, as a result of raids. The capture of weapons, ammunition and explosives is the urban guerrilla's goal in assaulting commercial businesses, industries and quarries.

**Liberation Of Prisoners**

The liberation of prisoners is an armed action designed to free jailed urban guerrillas. In daily struggle against the enemy, the urban guerrilla is subject to arrest, and can be sentenced to unlimited years in jail.

This does not mean that the battle ends here. For the guerrilla, his experience is deepened by prison, and struggle continues even in the dungeons where he is held. The imprisoned guerrilla views the prisons of the enemy as a terrain which he must dominate and understand in order to free himself by a guerrilla operation. There is no jail, either on an island, in a city penitentiary, or on a farm, that is impregnable to the slyness, cleverness and firepower of the rebels.

The urban guerrilla who is free views the jails of the enemy as the inevitable site of guerrilla actions designed to liberate his ideological comrades from prison. It is this combination of the urban guerrilla in freedom and the urban guerrilla in jail that results in the armed operations we refer to as "liberation of prisoners".

The guerrilla operations that can be used in liberating prisoners are the following;

1. riots in penal establishments, in correctional colonies or camps, or on transport or prison ships;

2. assaults on urban or rural prisons, detention centers, prison camps, or any other permanent or temporary place where prisoners are held;

3. assaults on prisoner transport trains or convoys;

4. raids and penetrations of prisons;

5. ambushing of guards who move prisoners.

## Executions

Execution is the killing of a foreign spy, of an agent of the dictatorship, of a police torturer, of a dictatorial personality in the government involved in crimes and persecutions against patriots, of a stool pigeon, informer, police agent or police provocateur. Those who go to the police of their own free will to make denunciations and accusations, who supply information and who finger people, must be executed when they are caught by the urban guerrillas.

Execution is a secret action, in which the least possible number of urban guerrillas are involved. In many cases, the execution can be carried out by a single sniper, patient, alone and unknown, and operating in absolute secrecy and in cold blood.

## Kidnapping

Kidnapping is capturing and holding in a secret place a spy, political personality or a notorious and dangerous enemy of the revolutionary movement. Kidnapping is used to exchange or liberate imprisoned revolutionaries or to force the suspension of torture in jail by the military dictatorship.

The kidnapping of personalities who are well-known artists, sports figures or who are outstanding in some other field, but who have evidenced no political interest, can be a useful form of propaganda for the guerrillas, provided it occurs under special circumstances, and is handled so the public understands and sympathizes with it. The kidnappings of foreigners or visitors constitutes a form of protest against the penetration and domination of imperialism in our country.

## Sabotage

Sabotage is a highly destructive type of attack using very few persons — and sometimes requiring only one — to accomplish the desired result. When the urban guerrilla uses sabotage, the first step is isolated sabotage. Then comes the step of dispersed and general sabotage, carried out by the population.

Well-executed sabotage demands study, planning and careful action. A characteristic form of sabotage is explosion, using dynamite, fire or the placing of mines. A little sand, a trickle of any kind of combustible, a poor lubrication job, a screw removed, a short circuit, inserted pieces of wood or iron, can cause irreparable damage.

The objective of sabotage is to hurt, to damage, to make useless and to destroy vital enemy points such as the following:

1. the economy of the country

2. agricultural or industrial production

3. transport and communication systems

4. military and police systems and their establishments and depots

5. the repressive military-police system

6. the firms and properties of exploiters in the country

The urban guerrilla should endanger the economy of the country, particularly its economic and financial aspects, such as its domestic and foreign banking network, its exchange and credit systems, its tax collection system, etc.

Public offices, centers of government and government depots are easy targets for sabotage. Nor will it be easy to prevent the sabotage of agricultural and industrial production by the urban guerrilla, with his thorough knowledge of the local situation.

Factory workers acting as urban guerrillas are excellent industrial saboteurs, since they, better than anyone, understand the industry, the factory, the machinery or the part most likely to destroy an entire operation, doing much more damage than a poorly-informed layman could do.

With respect to the enemy's transport and communications systems, beginning with railway traffic, it is necessary to attack them systematically with sabotage. The only caution is against causing death and injury to passengers, especially regular commuters on suburban and long-distance trains. Attacks on freight trains, rolling or stationary stock, stoppage of military transports and communciations systems, these are the major objectives in this area. Sleepers can be damaged and pulled up, as can rails. A tunnel blocked by a barrier of explosives, or an obstruction caused by a derailed car, causes enormous harm.

The derailment of a train carrying fuel is of major damage to the enemy. So is dynamiting a railroad bridge. In a system where the size and weight of the rolling equipment is enormous, it takes months for workers to repair or rebuild the destruction and damage.

As for highways, they can be obstructed with trees, stationary vehicles, ditches, dislocation of barriers by dynamite, and bridges destroyed by explosions.

Ships can be damaged at anchor in seaports or riverports, or in the shipyards. Aircraft can be destroyed or damaged on the ground.

Telephone and telegraph lines can be systematically damaged, their towers blown up, and their lines made useless. Transport and communications must be sabotaged immediately because the revolutionary movement has already begun in Brazil, and it is essential to impede the enemy's movement of troops and munitions.

Oil lines, fuel plants, depots for bombs and ammunition arsenals, military camps and bases must become targets for sabotage operations, while vehicles, army trucks and other military or police vehicles must be destroyed wherever they are found. The military and police repression centers and their specialized organs must also claim the attention of the guerrilla saboteur. Foreign firms and properties in the country, for their part, must become such frequent targets of sabotage that the volume of actions directed against them surpasses the total of all other actions against enemy vital points.

## Terrorism

Terrorism is an action, usually involving the placement of an explosive or firebomb of great destructive power, which is capable of effecting irreparable loss against the enemy. Terrorism requires that the urban guerrilla should have adequate theoretical and practical knowledge of how to make explosives.

The terrorist act, apart from the apparent ease with which it can be carried out, is no different from other guerrilla acts and actions whose success depends on planning and determination. It is an action which the urban guerrilla must execute with the greatest calmness and determination.

Although terrorism generally involves an explosion, there are cases in which it may be carried out through executions or the systematic burning of installations, properties, plantations, etc. It is essential to point out the importance of fires and the construction of incendiary devices such as gasoline bombs in the technique of guerrilla terrorism.

Another thing is the importance of the material the urban guerrilla can persuade the people to expropriate in the moments of hunger and scarcity brought about by the greed of the big commercial interests.

Terrorism is a weapon the revolutionary can never relinquish.

## Armed Propaganda

The coordination of urban guerrilla activities, including each armed action, is the primary way of making armed propaganda. These actions, carried out with specific objectives and aims in mind, inevitably become propaganda material for the mass communication system. Bank robberies, ambushes, desertions and the diverting of weapons, the rescue of prisoners, executions, kidnappings, sabotage, terrorism and the war of nerves are all cases in point.

Airplanes diverted in flight by guerrillla action, ships and trains assaulted and seized by armed guerrillas, can also be carried out solely for propaganda effect.

But the urban guerrilla must never fail to install a clandestine press, and must be able to turn out mimeographed copies using alcohol or electric plates and other duplicating apparatus, expropriating what he cannot buy in order to produce small clandestine newspapers, pamphlets, flyers and stamps for propaganda and agitation against the dictatorship.

The urban guerrilla engaged in clandestine printing facilitates enormously the incorporation of large numbers of people into the struggle, by opening a permanent work front for those willing to carry on propaganda, even when to do so means to act alone and risk their lives.

With the existence of clandestine propaganda and agitational material, the inventive spirit of the urban guerrilla expands and creates catapaults, artifacts, mortars and other instruments with which to distribute the anti-government propaganda at a distance.

Tape recordings, the occupation of radio stations, the use of loudspeakers, graffiti on walls and other inaccessible places are other forms of propaganda. A consistent propaganda by letters sent to specific addresses, explaining the meaning of the urban guerrilla's armed actions, produces considerable results and is one method of influencing certain segments of the population.

Even this influence—exercised in the heart of the people by every possible propaganda device, revolving around the activity of the urban guerrilla—does not indicate that our forces have everyone's support. It is enough to win the support of a portion of the population, and this can be done by popularizing the motto, "Let he who does not wish to do anything for the guerrillas do nothing against them."

## The War Of Nerves

The war of nerves or psychological warfare is an aggressive technique, based on the direct or indirect use of mass media and rumors in order to demoralize the government.

In psychological warfare, the government is always at a disadvantage because it imposes censorship on the media and winds up in a defensive position by not allowing anything against it to filter through. At this point, it becomes desperate, is involved in greater contradictions and loss of prestige, and loses time and energy in an exhausting effort at control which is liable to be broken at any moment.

The objective of the war of nerves is to mislead, spreading lies among the authorities in which everyone can participate, thus creating an atmosphere of nervousness, discredit, insecurity, uncertainty and concern on the part of the government.

The best methods used by urban guerrillas in the war of nerves are the following:

1. Using the telephone and the mail to announce false clues to the police and government, including information on the planting of bombs and any other act of terrorism in public offices and other places — kidnapping and assassination plans. etc. — to force the authorities to wear themselves out by following up on the false information fed to them;

2. Letting false plans fall into the hands of the police to divert their attention;

3. Planting rumors to make the government uneasy;

4. Exploiting by every means possible the corruption, the mistakes and the failures of the government and its representatives, forcing them into demoralizing explanations and justifications in the very communication media they wish to maintain under censorship;

5. Presenting denunciations to foreign embassies, the United Nations, the papal nunciature, and the international commissions defending human rights or freedom of the press, exposing each concrete violation and each use of violence by the military dictatorship and making it known that

the revolutionary war will continue with serious danger for the enemies of the population.

## How To Carry Out The Action

The urban guerrilla who correctly carries through his apprenticeship and training must give the greatest possible importance to his method of carrying out actions, for in this he cannot commit the slightest error. Any carelessness in learning tactics and their use invites certain disaster, as experience teaches us every day.

Common criminals commit errors frequently because of their tactics, and this is one of the reasons why the urban guerrillas must be so insistently preoccupied with following revolutionary tactics, and not the tactics of bandits. And not only for that reason. There is no urban guerrilla worthy of the name who ignores the revolutionary method of action and fails to practice it rigorously in the planning and execution of his activities.

"The giant is known by his toe." The same can be said of the urban guerrilla, who is known from afar by his correct tactics and his absolute fidelity to principle.

The revolutionary method of carrying out actions is strongly and forcefully based on the knowledge and use of the following elements;

1. investigation and intelligence gathering

2. observation and vigilance

3. reconnaissance, or exploration of the terrain

4. study and timing of routes

5. mapping

6. mechanization

7. careful selection of personnel

8. selection of firepower

9. study and practice in success

10. success

11. use of cover

12. retreat

13. dispersal

14. the liberation or transfer of prisoners

15. the elimination of evidence

l6. the rescue of wounded

## Some Observations On Tactics

When there is no information, the point of departure for planning the action must be investigation, observation and vigilance. This method produces good results.

In any event, even when there is information, it is essential to make observations to see that information is not at odds with observation or vice versa. Reconnaissance or exploration of the terrain and the study and timing of routes are so important that to omit them is to make a stab in the dark.

Mechanization, in general, is an underestimated factor in the tactics of conducting an action. Frequently, mechanization is left to the end, on the eve of the action, before anything is done about it. This is a mistake. Mechanization must be seriously considered. It must be undertaken with considerable foresight and with careful planning, based on careful and precise information. The care, conservation, maintenance and camouflaging of stolen vehicles are very important details of mechanization. When transportation fails, the primary action fails, with serious material and morale problems for the urban guerrillas.

The selection of personnel requires great care in order to avoid the inclusion of indecisive or wavering persons who present the danger of contaminating others, a danger that must be avoided.

The withdrawal is equally or more important than the operation itself, to the point that it must be rigorously planned, including the possibility of defeat.

One must avoid rescue or transfer of prisoners with children present, or anything to attract the attention of people passing through the area. The best thing is to make the rescue appear as natural as possible, winding through different routes or narrow streets that scarcely permit passage on foot, in order to avoid an encounter between two cars. The elimination of tracks is obligatory and demands the greatest caution—also in removing fingerprints and any other sign that could give the enemy information. Lack of care in the elimination of evidence is a factor that increases nervousness in our ranks, which the enemy often exploits.

## Rescue Of The Wounded

The problem of the wounded in urban guerrilla warfare merits special attention. During guerrilla operations in the urban area, it may happen that some comrade is wounded by the police. When a guerrilla in the firing group has a knowledge of first aid, he can do something for the wounded comrade on the spot. Under no circumstances should the wounded guerrilla be abandoned at the site of the battle or left in the enemy's hands.

One of the precautions we must take is to set up first-aid courses for men and women, courses in which guerrillas can learn the rudiments of emergency medicine. The urban guerrilla who is a doctor, nurse, med student, pharmacist or who simply has had first aid training is a necessity in modern guerrilla struggle. A small manual of first aid for urban guerrillas, printed on mimeographed sheets, can also be produced by anyone who has enough knowledge.

In planning and carrying out an armed action, the urban guerrilla cannot forget the organization of medical support. This must be accomplished by means of a mobile or motorized clinic. You can also set up a mobile first aid station. Another solution is to utilize the skills of a medical comrade, who waits with his bag of equipment in a designated house to which the wounded are brought.

The ideal would be to have our own well-equipped clinic, but this is very expensive unless we expropriate all of our materials.

When all else fails, it is often necessary to resort to legal clinics, using armed force if necessary to force a doctor to treat our wounded.

In the eventuality that we fall back upon blood banks to purchase blood or plasma, we must not use legal addresses and certainly no addresses where the wounded can really be found, since they are under our care and protection. Nor should we supply the addresses of those involved in the guerrilla organization to the hospitals and health care clinics where we may take them. Such caution is indispensable to covering our tracks.

The houses in which the wounded stay cannot be known to anyone but the small group of comrades responsible for their care and transport. Sheets, bloody clothing, medicine and any other indications of treatment of comrades wounded in combat must be completely eliminated from any place they visit to receive treatment.

## Guerrilla Security

The urban guerrilla lives in constant danger of the possibility of being discovered or denounced. The primary security problem is to make certain that we are well-hidden and well-guarded, and that there are secure methods to keep the police from locating us.

The worst enemy of the urban guerrilla, and the major danger that we run into, is infiltration into our organization by a spy or informer. The spy trapped within the organization will be punished with death. The same goes for those who desert and inform to the police.

A well-laid security means there are no spies or agents infiltrated into our midst, and the enemy can receive no information about us even through indirect means. The fundamental way to insure this is to be strict and cautious in recruiting. Nor is it permissible for everyone to know everything and everyone. This rule is a fundamental ABC of urban guerrilla security.

The enemy wants to annihilate us and fights relentlessly to find us and destroy us, so our greatest weapon lies in hiding from him and attacking by surprise.

The danger to the urban guerrilla is that he may reveal himself through carelessness or allow himself to be discovered through a lack of vigilance. It is impermissible for the urban guerrilla to give out his own or any other clandestine address to the police, or to talk too much.

Notations in the margins of newspapers, lost documents, calling cards, letters or notes, all these are evidence that the police never underestimate. Address and telephone books must be destroyed, and one must not write or hold any documents. It is necessary to avoid keeping archives of legal or illegal names, biographical information, maps or plans. Contact numbers should not be written down, but simply committed to memory.

The urban guerrilla who violates these rules must be warned by the first one who notes this infraction and, if he repeats it, we must avoid working with him in the future.

The urban guerrilla's need to move about constantly with the police nearby — given the fact that the police net surrounds the city — forces him to adopt various security precautions depending upon the enemy's movements. For this reason, it is necessary to maintain a daily information service about what the enemy appears to be doing, where the police net is operating and what points are being watched. The daily reading of the police news in the newspapers is a fountain of information in these cases.

The most important lesson for guerrilla security is never, under any circumstances, to permit the slightest laxity in the maintenance of security measures and precautions within the organization.

Guerrilla security must also be maintained in the case of an arrest. The arrested guerrilla must reveal nothing to the police that will jeopardize the organization. he must say nothing that will lead, as a consequence, to the arrest of other comrades, the discovery of addresses or hiding places, or the loss of weapons and ammunition.

## The Seven Sins Of The Urban Guerrilla

Even when the urban guerrilla applies proper tactics and abides by its security rules, he can still be vulnerable to errors. There is no perfect urban guerrilla. The most he can do is make every effort to diminish the margin of error, since he cannot be perfect. One of the means we should use to diminish the possibility of error is to know thoroughly the seven deadly sins of the urban guerrilla and try to avoid them.

The first sin of the guerrilla is inexperience. The urban guerrilla, blinded by this sin, thinks the enemy is stupid, underestimates the enemy's intelligence, thinks everything is easy and, as a result, leaves evidence that can lead to disaster.

Because of his inexperience, the urban guerrilla may also overestimate the forces of the enemy, believing them to be stronger than they really are. Allowing himself to be fooled by this presumption, the urban guerrilla becomes intimidated and remains insecure and indecisive, paralyzed and lacking in audacity.

The second sin of the urban guerrilla is to boast about the actions he has undertaken and to broadcast them to the four winds.

The third sin of the urban guerrilla is vanity. The guerrilla who suffers from this sin tries to solve the problems of the revolution by actions in the city, but without bothering about the beginnings and survival of other guerrillas in other areas. Blinded by success, he winds up organizing an action that he considers decisive and that puts into play the entire resources of the organization. Since we cannot afford to break the guerrilla struggle in the cities while rural guerrilla warfare has not yet erupted, we always run the risk of allowing the enemy to attack us with decisive blows.

The fourth sin of the urban guerrilla is to exaggerate his strength and to undertake actions for which he, as yet, lacks sufficient forces and the required infrastructure.

The fifth sin of the urban guerrilla is rash action. The guerrilla who commits this sin loses patience, suffers an attack of nerves, does not wait for anything, and impetuously throws himself into action, suffering untold defeats.

The sixth sin of the urban guerrilla is to attack the enemy when they are most angry.

The seventh sin of the urban guerrilla is to fail to plan things, and to act spontaneously.

## Popular Support

One of the permanent concerns of the urban guerrilla is his identification with popular causes to win public support. Where government actions become inept and corrupt, the urban guerrilla should not hesitate to step in and show that he opposes the government, and thus gain popular sympathy. The present government, for example, imposes heavy financial burdens and excessively high taxes on the people. It is up to the urban guerrilla to attack the dictatorship's tax collection system and to obstruct its financial activities, throwing all the weight of armed action against it.

The urban guerrilla fights not only to upset the tax collection system—the weapon of armed action must also be directed against those government agencies that raise prices and those who direct them as well as against the wealthiest of the national and foreign profiteers and the important property owners. In short, against all those who accumulate huge fortunes out of the high cost of living, the wages of hunger, excessive prices and high rents.

Foreign industries, such as refrigeration and other North American plants that monopolize the market and the manufacture of general food supplies, must be systematically attacked by the urban guerrillas.

The rebellion of the urban guerrilla and his persistance in intervening in political questions is the best way of insuring popular support for the cause which we defend. We repeat and insist on repeating—it is the way of insuring popular support. As soon as a reasonable portion of the population begins to take seriously the actions of the urban guerrilla, his success is guaranteed.

The government has no alternative except to intensify its repression. The police networks, house searches, the arrest of suspects and innocent persons, and the closing off of streets make life in the city unbearable. The military dictatorship embarks on massive political persecution. Political assassinations and police terror become routine.

In spite of all this, the police systematically fail. The armed forces, the navy and the air force are mobilized to undertake routine police functions, but even so they can find no way to halt guerrilla operations or to wipe out the revolutionary organization, with its fragmented groups that move around and operate throughout the country.

The people refuse to collaborate with the government, and the general sentiment is that this government is unjust, incapable of solving problems, and that it resorts simply to the physical liquidation of its opponents. The political situation in the country is transformed into a military situation in which the "gorillas" appear more and more to be the ones responsible for violence, while the lives of the people grow worse.

When they see the military and the dictatorship on the brink of the abyss, and fearing the consequences of a civil war which is already well underway, the pacifiers (always to be found within the ruling elite) and the opportunists (partisans of nonviolent struggle) join hands and circulate rumors behind the scenes begging the hangmen for elections, "re-democratization", constitutional reforms, and other tripe designed to fool the people and make them stop the rebellion.

But, watching the guerrillas, the people now understand that it is a farce to vote in any elections which have as their sole objective guaranteeing the survival of the dictatorship and covering up its crimes. Attacking wholeheartedly this election farce and the so-called "political solution", which is so appealing to the opportunists, the urban guerrillas must become even more aggressive and active, resorting without pause to sabotage, terrorism, expropriations, assaults, kidnappings, executions, etc.

This action answers any attempt to fool the people with the opening of Congress and the reorganization of political parties — parties of the government and of the positions which the government allows — when all the time parliament and the so-called "parties" only function thanks to the permission of the military dictatorship, in a true spectacle of puppets or dogs on a leash.


The role of the urban guerrilla, in order to win the support of the population, is to continue fighting, keeping in mind the interests of the people and heightening the disastrous situation within which the government must act. These are the conditions, harmful to the dictatorship, which permit the guerrillas to open rural warfare in the middle of an uncontrollable urban rebellion.

The urban guerrilla is engaged in revolutionary action for the people, and with them seeks the participation of the people in the struggle against the dictatorship and the liberation of the country. Beginning with the city and the support of the people, the rural guerrilla war develops rapidly, establishing its infrastructure carefully while the urban area continues the rebellion.